How to Crochet Baskets

Easy and Modern Crochet Storage Basket Patterns Step by Step Guide for Beginners

Copyright © 2021

All rights reserved.

DEDICATION

Contents

Simple Crochet Basket

Skill Level: Easy

MATERIALS

Super Bulky Yarn (6) I used Lion Brand Yarn Hometown USA in Chicago Charcoal

Size N 9.00 MM Crochet Hook

Yarn Needle

Scissors

Notes

Slip Stitch does not count as a chain when working in the round. (skip it)

Make sure to slip stitch to first Single or Double Crochet in each round not the Chain 1 or 2.

CROCHET PATTERN:

Round 1: Chain 3, 10 Double Crochets in 3rd Chain from hook. Slip Stitch to top of first Double Crochet.

Round 2: Chain 2, 2 Double Crochets in Each Chain Around. Slip Stitch to top of First Double Crochet (not the chain 2)

Round 3: Chain 2, 2 Double Crochets in first Stitch, *1 Double Crochet in next stitch, 2 Double Crochets in Next stitch, Repeat from * around until last chain, slip stitch to the top of the first Double Crochet.

Round 4: Chain 2, 1 Double Crochet in each stitch around. Slip Stitch to top of first Double Crochet.

Round 5 & 6: Repeat Round 4.

Round 7: Chain 2, Double Crochet in first st *Skip next stitch, Double Crochet in the next stitch, Now go back and Double Crochet in the Skipped stitch (creates a crisscross) Repeat from * until the end of round. Slip Stitch to top of first Double Crochet.

Round 8: Chain 1, Single Crochet in each stitch around. Slip stitch to top of first Single Crochet.

Round 9: Chain 1, Slip Stitch in ever stitch around. Fasten off. Weave in ends with Yarn needle

Finished Dimensions are approximately a 13 Inch Circumference and 5 Inch Height.

Bow: (optional)

Cut a 24 Inch Piece of Yarn with Scissors

Attach yarn to yarn needle

Weave in yarn completely around basket along top of Single Crochet round (see picture)

Pull yarn through as you are weaving it around until you are left with about 1 inch of space between yarn ends. (See picture)

Tie a bow and cut ends if you choose. It really depends on how long you want your bow.

The basket could also be easily cinched closed to hide gifts and make gift giving even more fun than it already is!

I ended up trimming the ends of the bow to make it a little shorter.

Which way do you prefer?

Bow?

or

No Bow?

Rainbow Storage Basket

Finished size: H 26cm (10.5"), D 32cm (12.5")

MATERIALS

1 large cone white T-shirt yarn (about 600g)

T-shirt yarn (or equivalent) in purple, pink, orange, yellow, green and blue (about 100g each) or 1 large cone of contrasting colour of choice.

12mm bamboo crochet hook

scrap of yarn for stitch marker

scissors

large tapestry needle for weaving in ends

CROCHET PATTERN:

Stitches used & Abbreviations – US terminology used

Magic loop

ch chain stitch

sc Single crochet (US) = double crochet (UK)

ss Slip Stitch

st(s) Stitch(s)

Pattern Notes:

This pattern is worked in the round (spiral), use a stitch marker or scrap of yarn to mark beginning of each row. White yarn will be carried up the inside of the basket from each working row, coloured yarn changes are in the style of tapestry crochet where the coloured yarn tail is crocheted over (by the white) for a few stitches before the colour starts and ends to secure. If you are working the stripes in one colour, do not break off, carry the yarn up the inside of the basket.

Because the basket is worked in a spiral the stripes will have a jog (where the colour jumps) in the start of each row, use an alternate jog free technique if this isn't pleasing to you.

Rows 1-11 in white (do not break off after row 11)

R1 – Make a Magic loop and sc 10 stitches into it (10st)

R2 – 2 sc into every st (20st)

R3 – (sc in next st, 2 sc in next st) around (30st)

R4 – (sc in next 2 sts, 2 sc in next st) around (40st)

R5 – sc into every st

R6 – (sc in next 3 sts, 2 sc in next st) around (50st)

R7 – sc into every st

R8 – (sc in next 4 sts, 2 sc in next st) around (60st)

R9 – sc into every st

R10 – (sc in next 5 sts, 2 sc in next st) around (70st)

R11 – sc into the back loop of every stitch (start weaving in next colour about 6 st before end of round)

Rows 12-29 are all the same – sc into every stitch in the following colour pattern

2x purple, 1x white, 2 x pink, 1x white, 2x orange, 1x white, 2x yellow, 1x white, 2x green, 1x white, 2x blue, 1x white

Row 30 – sc 14, ch 10 (skip 8 st), sc 27, ch 10 (skip 8 st), sc 13.

Row 31 – sc into every stitch, 10 sc over each chain section, sc to marker, ss and weave in ends.

Jewelry Catchers

MATERIALS

Size J 6.0 Crochet Hook (Note: if I made these again, I'd try with a smaller hook)

Super Bulky Yarn – I used Lion Brand Hometown USA in Houston Cream (white) and Phoenix Azalea (pink)

Scissors

Tapestry Needle to weave in ends

CROCHET PATTERN:

Small Basket Crochet Pattern (easier of the two baskets)

With your size J crochet hook, chain 3

Round 1 Sc 6 times into second chain from hook (mark your rounds if needed)

Round 2 Sc 2 times into each sc around (12 stitches)

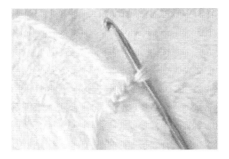

Round 3 *Sc 2 times into 1st sc, sc into next sc* Repeat around (18 stitches)

Round 4 *Sc 2 times into 1st sc, sc, sc* Repeat around (24 stitches)

Round 5 *Sc 2 times into 1st sc, sc, sc, sc* Repeat around (30 stitches)

Round 6 Sc around

Round 7 – until basket reaches 1 3/4 inches – 2" tall, sc in continuous rounds (no need to slip stitch to join)

Final Round – Change color to pink, sc around, slip stitch to join, tie off and weave in ends.

Large Basket Crochet Pattern

With your size J crochet hook and white yarn, chain 3

Round 1 Sc 6 into second chain from hook (place a stitch marker to mark the end of your round if you prefer – work in continuous rounds. No need to slip stitch to join)

Round 2 Sc 2 into each stitch around (12 stitches total)

Round 3 *Sc 2, sc 1* Repeat from * to * around (18 stitches total)

Round 4 *Sc 2, sc 1, sc1* Repeat around (24 stitches total)

Round 5 * Sc 2, sc 1, sc1, sc1* Repeat around (30 stitches)

Round 6 * Sc 2, sc 1, sc1, sc1, sc1* Repeat around (36 stitches)

Round 7 *Sc 2, sc 1, sc1, sc1, sc1, sc1* Repeat around (42 stitches)

Slip stitch in next stitch to join

Sides of Basket

Round 1 With same yarn, sc in front loop only around

Round 2 – until basket reaches 1.5 inches tall – work single crochet in continuous rounds

Next Round (Once basket is 1.5 inches tall) -Change color to pink – Sc in 1st stitch, *chain 1, skip stitch, sc in next stitch* (In other words, make a single crochet, then chain one, skip a stitch below and single crochet into the next stitch – repeat this around)

Next Round – Change color back to white, sc 2 times into each CHAIN stitch around (you are only working into the chain stitches below and single crocheting 2 times into each chain. Skip the single crochet stitches and ONLY work into the chain stitches)

Next Round and until basket reaches " 2 ¾ " inches tall TOTAL – single crochet in continuous rounds

Once entire basket measures approximately 2 ¾ " to 3" tall, skip stitch, slip stitch to join, tie off and weave in all ends.

Ombre Basket

Measurements

9.5 inches in height

12 inches in diameter

MATERIALS

9 different colors of worsted weight yarn

Size L crochet hook

Yarn needle

Pattern notes

The first ch 2 of each round counts as the first st

Hold 4 strands together

If you are using one color to make this basket, you will not need to join each rnd of the body of the basket. Continue working sc in a continuous spiral eliminating the seam.

You will work two rows of each of the colors except for the bottom and the last three rounds.

CROCHET PATTERN:

With Black (4 strands together)

Ch 3

Rnd 1: 7 hdc in 3rd ch from hook. Join with sl st (8 hdc)

Rnd 2: 2 hdc in each st. Join with sl st. (16 hdc)

Rnd 3: Ch 2, hdc in same st, hdc in next st, (2 hdc in next st, hdc in next st) around. Join with sl st. (24 hdc)

Rnd 4: Ch 2, hdc in same st, hdc in next 2 sts, (2 hdc in next st, hdc in next 2 sts) around. Join with sl st. (32 hdc)

Rnd 5: Ch 2, hdc in same st, hdc in next 3 sts, (2 hdc in next st, hdc in next 3 sts) around. Join with sl st. (40 hdc)

Rnd 6: Ch 2, hdc in same st, hdc in next 4 sts, (2 hdc in next st, hdc in next 4 sts) around. Join with sl st. (48 hdc)

Rnd 7: Ch 2, hdc in same st, hdc in next 5 sts, (2 hdc in next st, hdc in next 5 sts) around. Join. (56 hdc)

Rnd 8: Ch 2, hdc in same st, hdc in next 6 sts, (2 hdc in next st, hdc in next 6 sts) around. Join. (64 hdc)

Rnd 9: Ch 2, hdc in same st, hdc in next 7 sts, (2 hdc in next st, hdc in next 7 sts) around. Join. (72 hdc)

The next round will be the first row of the body of the basket. You will be working into the back of each hdc.

Rnd 10: Ch 1, sc under the line or ridge on the back of the first st of previous round. (Hdc have a line or ridge on the back of the stitch). You will be working under this line or ridge, not into the regular loops.

This will leave the two loops of the stitch

creating a seam separating the bottom and the sides of the basket.

Continue working sc around. Join with sl st.

Rnd 11: Ch 1, sc in same st and each st around. Join and finish off.

Rnd 12: With dark grey, sc in each st around. Join.

Rnd 13: Sc in each st around. Join and finish off.

Rnd 14-25: Repeat rounds 12-13.

Rnd 26: With mustard yellow (or the last color of choice), sc in each st around. Join.

Rnd 27: Sc in next 13 sts, ch 10, skip next 10 sts, sc in next 26 sts, ch 10, skip next 10 sts, sc in next 13 sts. Join.

Rnd 28: Sc in next 13 sts, 12 sc under the ch 10 sp. Sc in next 26 sts, 12 sc under the ch 10 sp, sc in next 13 sts. Join and finish off.

Weave ends.

Chunky Basket

MATERIALS

Hook: J (6.0 mm)

Tapestry needle to sew on accessories and hide the tails

Scissors to cut tails

Yarn: I used Lion Brand's Vanna White worsted weight yarn in Chocolate, Aqua, White, and Rose

Abbreviations

CH = chain

SC = single crochet

HDC = half double crochet

DC = double crochet

SL ST = slip stitch

st = stitch

Seed Stitch – 1 DC, 1 SC in the same space

CROCHET PATTERN:

Use TWO strands of worsted weight yarn at the same time for a chunky look, or one strand of a bulky yarn.

(Join each round with a SL ST, Each beginning CH of each round counts as that round's first stitch)

Ch 3, SL ST to form a circle

Round 1: (start with aqua) Ch 2, 7 HDC in ring (8 HDC total)

Round 2: Ch 2, HDC in same st, 2 HDC in each st around (16 HDC total)

Round 3: CH 2, 1 HDC in same st, 1 HDC in next st, *2 HDC in

27

next st, 1 HDC in next st* repeat from * around (24 HDC total)

Round 4: Ch 2, 1 HDC in same st, 1 HDC in each of the next 2 st's *2 HDC in next st, 1 HDC in each of the next 2 st's* repeat from * around (32 HDC total)

Round 5: Ch 2, 1 HDC in same st, 1 HDC in each of the next 3 st's, *2 HDC in next st, 1 HDC in each of the next 3 st's* repeat from * around (40 HDC total)

Round 6: Ch 2, 1 HDC in same st, 1 HDC in each of the next 4 st's, *2 HDC in next st, 1 HDC in each of the next 4 st's* repeat from * around (48 HDC total)

Round 7: Ch 2, 1 HDC in same st, 1 HDC in each of the next 5 st's, *2 HDC in next st, 1 HDC in each of the next 5 st's* repeat from * around (56 HDC total)

Round 8: Ch 2, 1 HDC in same st, 1 HDC in each of the next 5 st's, *2 HDC in next st, 1 HDC in each of the next 6 st's* repeat from * around (64 HDC total)

Round 9: Ch 2, 1 HDC in each st around (64 HDC total)

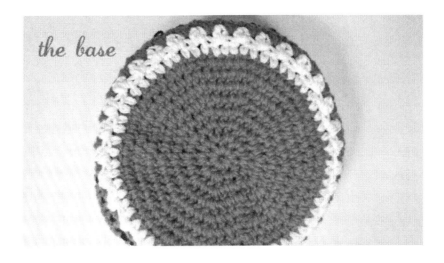

the base

Round 10: (switch to white) Ch 1, 1 HDC in each st around (64 HDC total)

Round 11-22: CH 3 (counts as 1st DC), 1 sc in the same space. Skip the next space. *Seed stitch in the next space. Skip the next space. repeat from * all the way around. (32 seed stitches total)

Round 23: (the handle) CH 3 (counts as 1st DC), 1 SC in the same space (counts as 1st Seed Stitch), 1 Seed Stitch in each of the next 13 spaces (14 Seed Stitches total). Skip the next 2 spaces & CH 6. 1 Seed Stitch in each of the next 14 spaces (14 seed stitches total). CH 6 & skip the last 2 spaces. Join with the beginning CH 3 with a SL ST. (28 seed stitches total)

Round 24: (switch to aqua) Attach the yarn (with a SL ST) to any place on the basket but the CH 6's. CH 2 (counts as first HDC). 1 HDC in each of the next 26 spaces (including the space in between the SC and DC in the seed stitches, 27 HDC total). 6 HDC on the CH 6. Repeat from * to complete the round (so, another 27 HDC, & 6 HDC on the CH 6).

Round 25: 1 HDC in each space around (66 HDC total)

This basket is really easy to make. I made it in 3 to 4 hours! It works up quickly because of the two strands of yarn.

Spikes Yarn Basket

Difficulty Level: Intermediate

Finished Size: Approximately 12 inches in diameter & 8 inches tall

MATERIALS

This basket is made using two strands of worsted weight yarn held together.

• Worsted weight yarn in 4 colors. Approximately 390 yards of the main color (CA) and small amounts of the rest.

• Size N (9mm) crochet hook

• Yarn needle for finishing

Yarns used in examples:

Green Basket: Loops & Threads Impeccable in Kelly Green(CA), Lion Brand Vanna's Choice in Dusty Rose (CB), Pink Poodle (CC), Pea Green (CD)

Gray Basket: Loops & Threads Impeccable in True Grey(CA), Lion Brand Vanna's Choice in Magenta (CB), Burgundy (CC), Honey (CD)

Techniques

● Invisible Join -An invisible join will be used at the end of a color, when you're about to start a new one. Here is a video tutorial: http://www.youtube.com/watch?v=bsHggQGFq3A

● Spike Stitch -On rnds 3, 6, 9, 12, 15, 18 spike stitches are used. In those rnds you will be instructed to "1 sc in st below next st." – this is the spike stitch. A spike stitch is simply a single crochet that is made in the previous rnd rather than the current one. If you were making a normal single crochet, you would put it where the X is in the photo below. Instead you will make it in the same stitch that that stitch is in, in the previous rnd, where the arrow is pointing in the photo below.

What you will do is insert your hook into that stitch (where the arrow is pointing, in the previous rnd), draw up a loop to the height of the current rnd and finish your single crochet as normal.

Abbreviations

sc- single crochet

dc – double crochet

hdc – half double crochet

ch – chain

sl st – slip stitch

rep – repeat

rnd – round

ea – each

sp – space

st/sts – stitch/stitches

FO – finish off

CA- Color A (main color)

CB, CC, CD- Color B,C,D

CROCHET PATTERN:

This pattern is worked in joined rounds. Join at the end of each round, when the pattern says to, using the type of join that round calls for.

Gauge is not critical, however if your gauge is different than mine, your basket will be larger or smaller than mine.

Gauge : 5 dc = 2 inches

You will be holding two strands of yarn together throughout the entire pattern.

Pattern

With CA:

rnd 1: ch 3 (counts as 1 dc). 13 dc in 3rd ch from hook. sl st to join. (14 dc)

rnd 2: ch 3 (counts as 1 dc). 1 dc in same st. 2 dc in ea st. invisible join & FO. (28 dc)

With CB:

rnd 3: ch 1 (does not count as a st). 1 sc in same st. 1 sc in ea of the next 2 sts. 1 sc in st below next st. [1 sc in ea of the next 3 sts. 1 sc in st below next st.] rep around. invisible join & FO. (28 sc)

With CA:

rnd 4: ch 3 (counts as 1 dc). 2 dc in next st. [1 dc in next st. 2 dc in next st.] rep around. sl st to join. (42 dc)

rnd 5: ch 3 (counts as 1 dc). 1 dc in next st. 2 dc in next st. [1 dc in ea of the next 2 sts. 2 dc in next st.] rep around. invisible join & FO. (56 dc)

With CC:

rnd 6: ch 1 (does not count as a st). 1 sc in same st. 1 sc in ea of the next 2 sts. 1 sc in st below next st. [1 sc in ea of the next 3 sts. 1 sc in st below next st.] rep around. invisible join & FO. (56 sc)

With CA:

rnd 7: ch 3 (counts as 1 dc). 1 dc in ea of the next 2 sts. 2 dc in next st. [1 dc in ea of the next 3 sts. 2 dc in next st.] rep around. sl st to join. (70 dc)

rnd 8: ch 3 (counts as 1 dc). 1 dc in ea of the next 3 sts. 2 dc in next st. [1 dc in ea of the next 4 sts. 2 dc in next st.] rep around. invisible join & FO. (84 dc)

With CD:

rnd 9: ch 1 (does not count as a st). 1 sc in same st. 1 sc in ea of the next 2 sts. 1 sc in st below next st. [1 sc in ea of the next 3 sts. 1 sc in st below next st.] rep around. invisible join & FO. (84 sc)

With CA:

rnd 10: ch 3 (counts as 1 dc). 1 dc in ea st. sl st to join. (84 dc)

rnd 11: ch 3 (counts as 1 dc). 1 dc in ea st. invisible join & FO. (84 dc)

With CB:

rnd 12: ch 1 (does not count as a st). 1 sc in same st. 1 sc in st below next st. [1 sc in ea of the next 3 sts. 1 sc in st below next st.] rep around. 1 sc in ea of the 2 remaining sts. invisible join & FO. (84 sc)

With CA:

rnds 13-14: rep rounds 10-11

With CC:

rnd 15: ch 1 (does not count as a st). 1 sc in same st. 1 sc in ea of the next 2 sts. 1 sc in st below next st. [1 sc in ea of the next 3 sts. 1 sc in st below next st.] rep around. invisible join & FO. (84 sc)

With CA:

rnds 16-17: rep rounds 10-11

With CD:

rnd 18: ch 1 (does not count as a st). 1 sc in same st. 1 sc in st below next st. [1 sc in ea of the next 3 sts. 1 sc in st below next st.] rep around. 1 sc in ea of the 2 remaining sts. invisible join & FO. (84 sc)

With CA:

rnd 19: ch 3 (counts as 1 dc). 1 dc in ea st. sl st to join. (84 dc)

rnd 20: ch 1 (does not count as a st). 1 sc in same st. ch 8. skip 8 sts. 1 sc in next st. 1 sc in ea of the next 33 sts. ch 8. skip 8 sts. 1 sc in next st. 1 sc in ea of the next 32 sts. sl st to join. (84)

rnd 21: ch 1 (does not count as a st). 1 sc in same st. 14 hdc in ch sp. 1 sc in ea of the next 33 sts. 14 hdc in ch sp. 1 sc in ea of the next 32 sts. invisible join & FO. (84)

rnd 1 & rnd 2

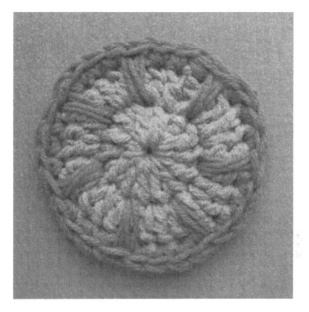

rnd 3 & rnd 5

rnd 6 & rnd 9

rnd 20 (making the handle)

rnd 21

T-Shirt Yarn Baskets

CROCHET PATTERN:

To start, a magic ring is created by wrapping the yarn around your fingers twice. Then hold the loop between your thumb and forefinger to start the foundation row.

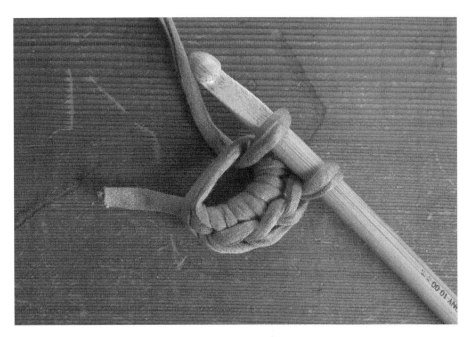

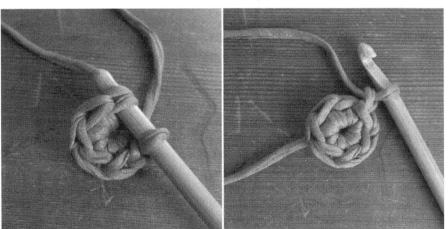

Row 1: ch1, dc 6 into a magic ring

After you've completed the 6 dc sts, pull the end yarn to tighten the loop.

slip stitch (sl st) at the end of the row. (You'll need to do this at the end of each row) after the last dc, insert your hook into the first stitch. Draw the yarn through both loops.

Honestly I always find the first sl st the hardest of all the rows, persevere its worth it!

Row 2: ch 1 (dc2 into each st) rpt 6 times, sl st to finish. You'll have a total of 12 sts, don't count the first chain as a stitch.

Row 3: ch1 (dc1, dc2 into the next st) rpt 6 times, sl st to finish. You'll have a total of 18 sts

Row 4: ch1 (dc2, dc2 into the next st) rpt 6 times, sl st to finish. You'll have a total of 24 sts

Row 5: ch1 (dc3, dc2 into the next st) rpt 6 times, sl st to finish. You'll have a total of 30 sts

Can you see the pattern forming. I get excited at this point. The base is almost complete.

AHHH, not so excited, i've hit a snag. This is part and parcel of recycled/ repurposed yarns. it happens. It's an easy fix and won't show up in your final product.

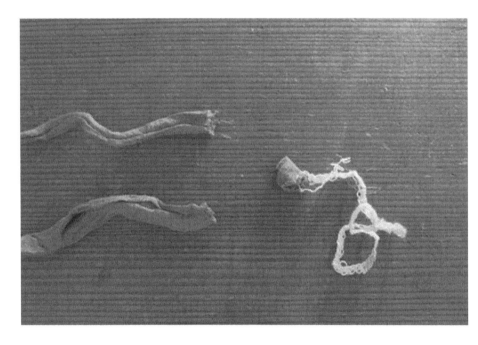

Untie the knot and cut off any scrap ends you don't need. Always try and minimise your waste if you can.

With your working yarn start the next dc st, but don't draw the final yarn through the two loops.

Instead draw the new yarn through the two loop to complete the st.

Now hold the two end yarns against your work as you continue to work the row. I am a big believer in tidying my ends up as I go. Purely driven by my strong dislike of weaving in ends.

Keep the ends in the

Stop and take a look at your work. You shouldn't see a significant difference between your stitches. Have a look at the font and back images. 3 stitches have been worked since adding the new yarn.

I usually only hide the yarn between 4/5 stitches, I haven't found I need any more than that.

Keep the ends dangling as you continue to work the row. they can be cut off later on. Don't cut them too early incase they pop up through your work

Now... back to the pattern.

Row 6- 9: ch1, dc into each st, sl st to finish. You'll have a total of 30 sts

Can you see, by not increasing the edges will start the curl up. They may need a little coaxing but as you continue to work the rows even, the walls will be easier to manipulate.

I wanted a shallow basket, but by all mean keep going taller if you have the yarn and desire a taller/ deeper basket.

At the end of the final row. Don't sl st to finish. Cut the yarn to a length of approx 6 inches. Pull the yarn through so there's no loop.

Either use a big tapestry needle or your hook to draw the yarn through the back of the first st.

I like to start at the back, but it doesn't matter whether you start back to front or front to back. Just mirror the instructions, if you choose to go the other way.

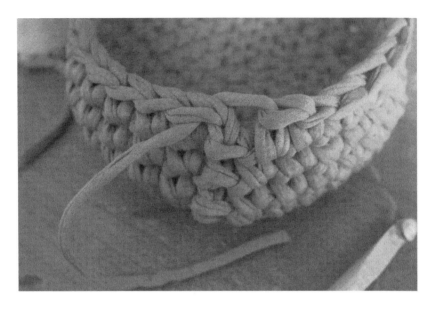

To complete the loop, now draw the yarn from the top, through the front loop of the last st.

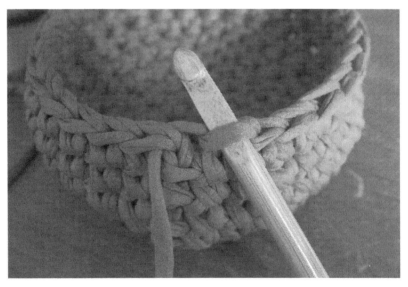

Ta da! Looks great doesn't it! My favourite way to finish a basket. Finish by weaving in that final end and the first end from the magic loop.

Trim all ends.

Rectangular Basket

MATERIALS

2 colors T-shirt yarn, approx. 160 yd each (I used 2 skeins of Fab-U-Loop yarn)

US N-P / 10 mm crochet hook

scissors

This pattern is written in U.S. crochet terms and abbreviations. Resources and tutorials you may find helpful in following this pattern: Crochet Abbreviations, U.S. to U.K. Crochet Conversion

Chart.

Add this pattern to your Ravelry library.

CROCHET PATTERN:

LARGE RECTANGULAR CROCHET BASKET PATTERN

Finished basket measures approximately 11 in. long × 8 in. wide × 4¾ in. tall.

Bottom

With CA, ch 11.

Row 1: Work 1 sc in 2nd ch from hook and each ch across, turn — 10 sts.

Row 2: Ch 1 (does not count as st here and througout), work 1 sc in each st across, turn — 10 sts.

Rows 3 through 19: Repeat Row 2, do not fasten off.

Upper

Round 1: Continuing with CA, ch 1, work 1 sc in each st across, work 1 sc on the edge of each row along the side, work 1 sc in each st across, work 1 sc on the edge of each row along remaining side, join and fasten off CA — 58 sts.

Round 2: Join CB in same st as join, ch 1, work 1 sc in same st as join and each st around, join — 58 sts.

Round 3: Ch 1, work 1 sc in same st as join and each st around, join — 58 sts.

Rounds 4 through 6: Repeat Round 3.

Round 7: Ch 1, work 1 sc in same st as join and in each of the next 2 sts, ch 6, skip next 4 sts, 1 sc in each of the next 25 sts, ch 6, skip next 4 sts, 1 sc in each of the next 22 sts, join and fasten off CB — 50 sts and 2 ch-6 loops.

Round 8: Join CA in same st as join, ch 1, work 1 sc in same st as join and in each of the next 2 sts, work 8 sc around ch-6 loop, 1 sc in each of the next 25 sts, work 8 sc around ch-6 loop, 1 sc in each of the next 22 sts, join and fasten off — 66 sts.

Weave in ends.

SMALL RECTANGULAR CROCHET BASKET PATTERN

Finished basket measures approximately 10 in. long × 7 in. wide × 4 in. tall.

Bottom

With CB, ch 9.

Row 1: Work 1 sc in 2nd ch from hook and each ch across, turn — 8 sts.

Row 2: Ch 1 (does not count as st here and througout), work 1 sc in each st across, turn — 8 sts.

Rows 3 through 17: Repeat Row 2, do not fasten off.

Upper

Round 1: Continuing with CB, ch 1, work 1 sc in each st across, work 1 sc on the edge of each row along the side, work 1 sc in each st across, work 1 sc on the edge of each row along remaining side, join and fasten off CB — 50 sts.

Round 2: Join CA in same st as join, ch 1, work 1 sc in same st as join and each st around, join — 50 sts.

Round 3: Ch 1, work 1 sc in same st as join and each st around, join — 50 sts.

Rounds 4 through 5: Repeat Round 3.

Round 6: Ch 1, work 1 sc in same st as join and in next st, ch 5, skip next 4 sts, 1 sc in each of the next 21 sts, ch 5, skip next 4 sts, 1 sc in each of the next 19 sts, join and fasten off CA — 42 sts and 2 ch-5 loops.

Round 7: Join CB in same st as join, ch 1, work 1 sc in same st as join and in next st, work 7 sc around ch-5 loop, 1 sc in each of the next 21 sts, work 7 sc around ch-5 loop, 1 sc in each of the next 19 sts, join and fasten off — 56 sts.

Weave in ends.

Made in the USA
Columbia, SC
17 November 2023

26690023R00038